CONJUNTO

CONJUNTO

VOZ DEL PUEBLO, CANCIONES DEL CORAZÓN

VOICE OF THE PEOPLE, SONGS FROM THE HEART

PHOTOGRAPHS BY JOHN DYER

PREFACE AND CAPTIONS BY JUAN TEJEDA

INTRODUCTION BY JOE NICK PATOSKI

UNIVERSITY OF TEXAS PRESS ✦ AUSTIN

The publication of this book was made possible,
in part, by a grant from Anheuser-Busch.

Requests for permission to reproduce material
from this work should be sent to:

Permissions
University of Texas Press
P.O. Box 7819
Austin, TX 78713-7819
www.utexas.edu/utpress/about/bpermission.html

∞ The paper used in this book meets the minimum requirements
of ANSI/NISO Z39.48-1992 (R1997) (Permanence of Paper).

Library of Congress Cataloging-in-Publication Data

Dyer, John, 1947–
Conjunto / photographs by John Dyer ; introduction by Joe Nick
Patoski ; preface and captions by Juan Tejeda. — 1st ed.
p.   cm.
ISBN 0-292-70931-5 (hardcover : alk. paper)
1. Conjunto music — Pictorial works.
2. Mexican Americans — Music — History and criticism — Portraits.
3. Musicians — Portraits.
I. Patoski, Joe Nick, 1951–
II. Tejeda, Juan, 1953–
III. Title.

ML3481.D94 2005
782.42164'089'6872073 — dc22
2004028730

All song lyrics © and reproduced with permission
San Antonio Music Publishers
P.O. Box 37250 San Antonio, Texas 78237

All photographs are by John Dyer, with the following exceptions:
Pages 2, 6: personal collection of Santiago Jiménez Jr.
Page 8 (Bruno Villarreal): public domain.
Page 8 (Santiago Jiménez Sr. and Lorenzo Caballero):
    personal collection of Santiago Jiménez Jr.
Page 9: public domain.

Jacket and book design by DJ Stout and
Julie Savasky, Pentagram Design, Austin, Texas

CONTENTS

THE PHOTOGRAPHS BY JOHN DYER   1

PREFACE BY JUAN TEJEDA   2

INTRODUCTION BY JOE NICK PATOSKI   6

PORTRAITS   12

ON THE SCENE   102

ACKNOWLEDGMENTS   121

THE PHOTOGRAPHS

BY JOHN DYER

I fell in love with conjunto music fifteen years ago. It was at the conjunto festival that my old friend Juan Tejeda used to put on at Rosedale Park in San Antonio.

My roots are German-Irish and I'm originally from Montana, but I've lived in San Antonio a long time. I didn't know all that much about this compelling, lively, danceable music I was hearing and seeing. But I love the incredibly rich Mexican cultural tradition and its influence here in South Texas.

Being a visual type, I was first drawn to the instruments: the lead accordion, colorful, lightweight, expressive, with buttons, not keys; a sideman playing a beautiful handmade two-tone guitar called a *bajo sexto*. The accordion and bajo sexto were accompanied by an electric bass and drums. The music was basic and clean. Polkas, waltzes, schottisches . . . musical rhythms familiar from my German heritage but also *boleros, rancheras, huapangos,* and *cumbias* from Mexico . . . a very interesting mix.

The men who play this music (and let's face it, there are very few women in the man's world of conjunto) are incredible, mostly self-taught musicians playing unbelievable riffs on the accordion and providing rock-solid rhythm with the other instruments. Most of the conjuntos are composed of working class folks who play for the sheer love of the music and a very real calling to keep this pure roots music alive for future generations.

Not long after that, I asked Tejeda for a list of ten to twelve of the most important conjunto musicians here in San Antonio and, using his name, I was able to make appointments and take portraits of them. For several years I would show these portraits around. I always got a good response and a lot of interest in who these folks were and what their music was like.

About a year ago it dawned on me that no one had ever done a book of photographs of the conjunto music scene: the *maestros* who play the music, the folks who come to dance to it. I knew I needed Joe Nick Patoski and Juan Tejeda to write about the music. They know everything about it, where it comes from, why it's important. I wanted to show my respect and admiration for the music and honor the people who perform it.

From the beginning Tejeda and I had a hard time deciding who should be in the book. We drew a pretty quick distinction between conjunto (a homegrown South Texas roots music) and norteño (indigenous to northern Mexico). Both kinds of music share certain qualities, but we felt that conjunto is distinctive enough to warrant its own overview.

There will, of course, be those who differ with our choices for portraits. Everyone I talk to who knows about conjunto music has his/her own favorites. It's not a neutral subject. So much of what makes folks like one musician over another is dependent on whether they go to their dances, whether they're related to them, whether their parents danced to their music way back when.

The portraits in this book are the ones I was able to get. A lot of them are from here in San Antonio, which is a center for the music. Regrettably, there are some giants of conjunto I was unable to get (Narciso Martínez, Tony de la Rosa, Don Santiago Jiménez) because they had passed on. But I did manage to photograph several *maestros* who have since passed on (Valerio Longoria, Fred Zimmerle, Juan Viesca, Daniel Garcés).

This book cannot be definitive. There are young musicians out there right now, making their mark on this music, who will deserve to be honored in a book of their own someday.

I dedicate this book to the conjunto musicians, old and young, who play for the joy of playing the music their parents and grandparents played or danced to. Not many of them will ever get rich performing this music, but they and we are the richer for it.

PREFACE

BY JUAN TEJEDA

A publicity photo of Tony de la Rosa from the 1960s. His style of accordion, played always for his people, was uniquely his own, never emulated.

Lunes, 7 de junio, 2004
12:41 en la mañana
Murió Tony de la Rosa este miércoles pasado,
2 de junio, en el año dos mil y cuatro. The world will never be the same without him in it, without him playing his accordion and singing his songs for the people. We lost a great man, a legend, a pioneer. The conjunto world is in mourning. *Tony era puro corazón.*

I wrote this journal entry the day after I had attended Tony's funeral service on Saturday, June 5, at the First Assembly of God Church in Kingsville, Texas. This is the most significant thing that has happened in conjunto music since, well, probably since Valerio Longoria died on December 15, 2000. "They're all dying," I told my *primo* Armando, who plays *bajo sexto*, as we were driving down to Tony's funeral service. "All of the early conjunto greats are dying." I told him that out of the six individuals we had inducted into the Conjunto Music Hall of Fame at the very first Tejano Conjunto Festival en San Antonio in 1982, only Esteban Jordán is alive. The other five, Santiago Jiménez Sr., Pedro Ayala, Narciso Martínez, Valerio Longoria, and now Tony de la Rosa, were dead. These were the people that established the conjunto tradition amongst the Mexican/Chicano people here in Texas. Conjunto lives because of them. And though they are gone, they will never die because their legacy lives on, and their *música, que está grabada en la memoria colectiva y el corazón del pueblo,* lives on.

I believe it was the great Chicano scholar Américo Paredes, *que en paz descanse,* that first said that much of our folklore here on the U.S.-Mexico border in Texas was a result of the intercultural conflict between Anglos and Mexicans. Manuel Peña, the foremost authority and theoretician on conjunto and Tejano music, agrees with Paredes and states that the Mexican-American War, which ended in 1848, "marks a turning point in the social, cultural, and economic transformation of the Southwest" and that "the conflict between Anglos and Mexicans was particularly violent in Texas," which in turn led to unique and expressive Mexican/Chicano cultural responses such as *corridos,* and the ensembles and styles of music known as conjunto and *orquesta Tejana.* Conjunto music was created out of this conflict and is at once a resolution and a synthesis.

The Spanish word *conjunto* simply means "ensemble," or "group." For many of the Mexican/Chicano people living in South Texas and other parts of the United States, however, conjunto refers to a specific Texas Mexican musical group, and style of music, whose principal instrument is the button accordion. The *mexicanos* living in South Texas and Northern Mexico adopted the button accordion from the German settlers during the late 1800s and began playing the lively and danceable polkas, waltzes, schottishes, redowas, and mazurkas. After the turn of the century, the accordion was paired up with the Spanish/Mexican *bajo sexto* (twelve-string bass rhythm guitar), and the creation of a new, original American musical ensemble and style of music was in the making. Conjunto fuses the German and the Mexican, accordion and *bajo sexto,* polkas and *huapangos,* the Old World and the New World. The modern standard, traditional four-piece conjunto consists of the accordion, *bajo sexto,* bass, and drums. Progressive conjuntos sometimes add keyboards, saxophone(s), or other instruments. The conjunto repertoire is varied with traditional instrumentals, rhythms, and *canciones,* combined with international influences. Conjunto is Chicano roots music. It is our history, our stories and poems in song. It is our bilingual/bicultural, multilingual/multicultural reality in music that combines *cumbias* and polkas *con elementos de* blues, country, rock, rap, reggae, salsa, merengue, jazz, and more. Conjunto music is at once *bien barrio* and beyond barriers and borders. Born out of the poor *mexicanos* in the *ranchos* of South Texas, conjunto music has become a powerful source of pride, Chicano self-identity, cultural reaffirmation, and empowerment. *Conjunto es comunidad:* our sacred Saturday night celebrations and ceremonies *donde la raza* dances in a circle, counter-

clockwise, always coming back to the source of the music, to the band, to the beat. *Conjunto es la voz del pueblo, y nuestras canciones vienen del corazón.*

Valerio Longoria, button accordionist extraordinaire, stylist, innovator, composer, vocalist, and recording artist who is considered one of the geniuses of conjunto music, once told me that his father bought him his first, used Hohner accordion from a pawn shop for $10 when he was seven years old.

I first met Valerio when he had just arrived from California in late 1980 and he was playing at the Club Íntimos just south of downtown San Antonio on Flores Street. I was amazed at the distinctive way in which he played his unique, deeper, octave-sounding accordion. His *pasadas* were original, fluid, and utilized the full range of music available to him on the melody side of the button board. His heartfelt *boleros* were some of the most romantic songs and beautiful music I had ever heard. I was already playing the accordion with my band, Conjunto Aztlan, but after hearing Valerio play that night, I commented to the friends that were with me that evening that I wanted to learn how to play the accordion like Valerio Longoria. He and I became *camaradas* that night and would remain so until his death.

I was already the Xicano Music Program Director for the Guadalupe Cultural Arts Center when I met Valerio, and in 1981 I hired him to be the first master accordion instructor at the center. He taught there for twenty years, and well over a thousand students, both young and old, including myself, learned at the hands of the master. I am proud to say that besides being

The drive among conjunto musicians to preserve and pass on their music is very strong. Here a student at the Conjunto Heritage Taller (workshop) in San Antonio warms up before attending a class taught by Bene Medina.

my *camarada,* Valerio was also my *maestro* and mentor.

Valerio Longoria y su conjunto was the only band to perform the first nineteen years in a row at the Tejano Conjunto Festival, where he also presented his accordion students in recital. For more than sixty years (he was almost seventy-six years old when he died), Valerio performed at dances across the United States, from Texas to Chicago, to Florida, to California. He performed at baptisms, birthday parties, *quinceañeras, bodas,* burials, festivals, and various other cultural celebrations. He played for rich and poor alike, sometimes for $2,000 a night, sometimes for $200. But it wasn't about the money for Valerio. He played because he loved his music and he loved his *raza.* He loved to perform for his people. He played and sang with such *corazón* and *emoción* that many times I saw him cry onstage, of joy and pain and *pasión de vivir.*

On June 26, 2004, the Conjunto Heritage Taller and Palo Alto College Conjunto Music Program, where I now work, joined forces with various community organizations such as KEDA Radio and *La Prensa de San Antonio,* to present the First Valerio Longoria Memorial Festival at Rosedale Park in San Antonio. The purpose of the festival was to raise money to purchase and place a fitting monument at Valerio's gravesite, and to establish the Valerio Longoria Conjunto Scholarship Fund for young conjunto students, a living tribute, we felt, for the man, his music, and his legacy. Among the fifteen bands that contributed their time and talent were conjunto greats Los Pavos Reales, Eddie "Lalo" Torres and Salvador García, Bene Medina y el Conjunto Águila, Nick Villarreal y su conjunto, and Los Pioneers de Ramz Guerrero. Valerio's son, Flavio Longoria, and grandson, Valerio Longoria IV, who perform as Los Longoria, closed out the dance. One of the highlights of the evening was when Robert Casillas, a thirteen-year-old former Valerio student and conjunto prodigy, performed with Bene Medina's band. Robert began taking accordion lessons with Valerio when he was seven years old. Not to be outdone, Cristina, Robert's nine-year-old little sister, who had first taken accordion lessons with Santiago Jiménez Jr. and was then studying with Bene Medina, took the stage next and blew away the awed and appreciative audience.

■

There's a scene in the classic Tejano music documentary film done by Hector Galán, *Songs of the Homeland,* that opens with a shot of the South Texas landscape, *grillos* buzzing, mesquite trees and a barbed-wire fence in the foreground, with cattle in the distance, and Tony de la Rosa is narrating: "One thing I'm real proud of is my style of music. *De aquí,* from here, from this area, from this piece of land here." During this narration, the scene cuts to another shot of the land, this time with *nopales* and a windmill, then a shot of Tony looking out over the land as he says: "To me, *el gusto, el gusto de producir esta música, viene del corazón."* The scene shifts again to a tight shot of Tony's hands putting his accordion into its case while narrating: "It's not what you play, but who you play for. And I figure that I play for my people"— tight shot of Tony's face while he's talking with tears in his eyes—"for the people that were born and raised with this certain type of feeling in them that I was lucky enough to have been a part of." Fade to black.

■

I'm kneeling in the church aisle right in front of Tony de la Rosa's open casket. His wife, Lucy, is sitting in the pew to my immediate left, and his brother, Adán, Tony's long-time *bajista* and *voz segunda,* sits in a wheelchair to my immediate right. I've come up to the very front because they started playing a video, on a small TV monitor placed on the stage right next to the casket, of Tony's final performance. He played at the wedding of his great-nephew Danny de la Rosa on May 15 at the Knights of Columbus Hall in Kingsville. This was a little over two weeks before his death on June 2. I do not want to remember Tony the way he's lying there, *bien flaco, en su ataúd.* I want to remember Tony the way I knew him best, the way we all knew him best,

playing his *acordeón* and singing for his people. After saying a few words, Tony breaks into his classic polka "Atotonilco," then medleys into a *canción ranchera,* "El muchacho alegre." *Gritos* can be heard throughout the dance hall. This is the Tony de la Rosa I know and will always remember: smiling, with his hat and glasses on, playing his *acordeón* in the style that he created and that only he could play, though many tried to emulate it. And even though he was skinny and gaunt, he didn't miss a lick on that ol' squeezebox, his music and spirit shining through brightly, bigger than life, bigger than death, *una estrella reluciente cantando "yo soy el muchacho alegre, del cielo favorecido,"* as his *familia,* his *raza,* danced to his polkas, *tirando gritos y bailando juntos* in a circle.

■

Unfortunately, Tony de la Rosa's photo is not included in this collection. He died before John Dyer had a chance to photograph him. This, however, underscores the importance of this historic book. Never before has there been a book that is devoted to photographs, portraits, really, of many of conjunto's all-time greats. Some of them, such as Valerio Longoria, Fred Zimmerle, and Daniel Garcés, have already passed on to the spirit world. We're lucky their images are on these pages, so that we can look at their strong mestizo/Chicano faces, remember them, remember their music, and honor them. Others are still very much alive and playing their infectious, foot-stompin', accordion-fueled music at dance halls and stages across South Texas and around the world. John Dyer has stopped time in these photos, capturing these amazing, trailblazing conjunto musicians in intimate moments where they work, play, and live. This is a rare opportunity for us to get to know them, at least a little. Look into their eyes. Enter their humble homes. *Wátchate el tandito, la guayabera, los* blue jeans, boots, cowboy hats, and Stacy Adams shoes. Check out how they caress their accordions and finger that *bajo sexto.* Listen to the music and feel the songs that pass through your fingertips as you turn these pages.

The primary instruments in a conjunto are the colorful, lively button accordion (top), which provides the focal point both musically and visually, and the *bajo sexto* guitar (bottom), which can hold either six or twelve strings. The *bajo sexto* provides the rhythm for the music and allows the accordionist to concentrate just on playing the melody of the song. This *bajo sexto* was hand-made in San Antonio by second-generation craftsman Alberto Macías.

INTRODUCTION

BY JOE NICK PATOSKI

Agapito Zúñiga, from a publicity still taken in the late 1950s. Unlike the majority of conjunto accordionists, Agapito played a key accordion as well as one with buttons. He no longer plays, preferring to pursue a religious calling.

The Spanish word *conjunto,* translated into English, literally means "group." In the Latin music world, the word is applied to an assembly of musicians smaller in number than an *orquesta* and larger than a duo.

When defining a style of music, though, conjunto is very specific. It refers to the indigenous music of mostly rural, working class Texas Mexicans, one and two generations removed from the other side of the U.S.-Mexico border. This interpretation of conjunto bears striking similarities to norteño music of northern Mexico and the *grupo* sound emanating from Monterrey, Nuevo León. Elements of conjunto are sometimes infused into contemporary Tejano music, the modern regional sound popular among more assimilated Mexican Americans in Texas and the southwestern United States. But conjunto, the germinating seed of what the general population often refers to as Tex-Mex, is clearly a sound unto itself.

Though little known outside the comfort zone where Texas Mexicans live, work, and dance, conjunto dates back to the mid-nineteenth century and the earliest waves of European immigrants arriving in Texas. The *mexicanos* already here paid close attention to the music the new arrivals played at dances. In the process they created a sound of their own.

Conjunto remains a vital cultural touchstone for a significant segment of the Mexican American community in Texas, no matter how urbane or Americanized they have become. It is heard throughout a region stretching from the Rio Grande to the Brazos River and beyond, emanating from restaurants, bars, dance halls, icehouses, parks, flea markets, television commercials, radio programs, sound systems in slow moving cars, and backyards.

San Antonio is its spiritual capital and commercial center, though conjunto's sphere of influence has become global. For while it may be a Tex-Mex thing, the sound and the compelling nature of its true-story songs and sad romance ballads sung in the heartbreak key long ago transcended its traditional cultural, social, and linguistic limitations. Since the 1970s conjunto has managed to subtly insinuate itself into American country, American rock, Mexican regional, Latin international, and American and European folk music sounds. In fact, conjunto has become so trendy, teenagers in Tokyo have formed their own conjuntos to emulate the sound.

That crossover appeal is underscored by some of the material in the typical conjunto band's repertoire. Even when sung *en español* and revved up considerably, what can be more American than "Beer Barrel Polka," "Open Up Your Heart and Let My Love Come In," "In Heaven, There Is No Beer," "Release Me," or even "Fraulein"?

Knowledge of Spanish and an understanding of the culture were missing when conjunto first entered the ears of a bored North Texas teenager aimlessly flipping around the radio dial forty years ago. I didn't have a clue what the vocalists were saying, but I could immediately recognize that whatever they were saying was being stated in such a compelling, passionate fashion, and being sung in front of an ensemble that played so amazingly tight and solid and heavy on the beat, I couldn't help but get hooked.

The siren's call of *el acordeón* working counterpoint against the thick chunks of backbeat strummed on the bajo sexto was irresistible. The sound floated and rose the same way thick air does during the long, hot Texas summer, informed by a sense of place I fully appreciated. Conjunto's heat, though, was a spontaneous combustion caused by a wicked conspiracy between a diatonic button accordion, a bajo sexto twelve-string guitar, and two vocalists harmonizing in Spanish and occasionally English, pushed by a syncopated beat pounded out with military precision.

The melody was familiar enough; the music's roots were firmly planted in the European polka. But this was like no polka I'd heard before. The rhythm pushing the song was too jaunty, too jumping, too Latino. It made

me want to dance. I figured out right then and there why some old-timers called conjunto *música alegre*— happy music. Joy permeated every note.

A better understanding came at Sunday *bailes* at *el club* Rockin' M, a country dance hall between Austin and Lockhart during the early 1970s. As I was sitting, listening, watching, drinking, and dancing among four generations of families, conjunto revealed itself as a community glue that held together people who were Mexican in heritage, Texan in outlook, and wholly original. Nowhere but Texas. This was authentic folk music—one of the last places left in America where real folks were making real music, performing in front of folks just like themselves.

I was hardly the only white guy to notice.

On several occasions, Flaco Jiménez's band from San Antonio included a guest player from Los Angeles named Ry Cooder. He was a renowned guitarist and

Flaco Jiménez at home with his first Grammy. Flaco was the first conjunto musician to achieve genuine international fame. He's recorded with, among others, the Texas Tornadoes, Doug Sahm, Dwight Yoakum, Emmylou Harris, the Rolling Stones, Buck Owens, and Los Super Seven.

The blind Bruno Villarreal in his later years. Bruno is credited with making the first recordings of conjunto music in the 1920s.

recording artist who recognized conjunto's uniqueness and set about learning it by doing an extended apprenticeship to master one of conjunto's essential ingredients, the *bajo sexto.*

Many dances at the Rockin' M were highlighted by accordion shootouts, most frequently between Flaco Jiménez, Agapito Zúñiga, El Escorpión de Corpus (the Scorpion of Corpus Christi), and Mingo Saldívar aka the Conjunto Cowboy, also from San Antonio. Jiménez was and is one of the genre's greatest stylists as well as the person most responsible for exporting the tradition beyond its traditional boundaries through his recordings with Doug Sahm and, later, the Texas Tornadoes, Dwight Yoakum, Emmylou Harris, the Rolling Stones, and Buck Owens, among others. Zúñiga was an elder, one of the old guard, well versed in the traditions of the music. Saldívar was the wild card, a middle-aged crazy who replaced Jiménez in Los Caporales, way back when, and who

Santiago Jiménez Sr. and Lorenzo Caballero near where they lived at La Piedrera (Cementville), a giant lime-stone quarry in what is now the middle of San Antonio.

carved out a following from his Spanish language covers of country music chestnuts such as "Ring of Fire" (made famous by Johnny Cash), refashioned, naturally, into a *polkita.*

The three would trade riffs back and forth with flourishes that became increasingly flamboyant and flashy until finally Mingo *Pingo* would start playing his instrument above his head and behind his back, and shut down the competition.

I'd learned about Flaco Jiménez through Doug Sahm, the rock and roller from San Antonio who had pop hits in the 1960s as leader of the Sir Douglas Quintet with songs rooted in a conjunto backbeat. In the early 1970s Sahm recorded two comeback albums with a superstar lineup of guest musicians including folk troubadour Bob Dylan and New Orleans keyboardist and composer Dr. John. The guest who caught my ear was Jiménez, Sahm's old compadre from El West Side.

Flaco turned me on to "Viva Seguin," the peppy polka instrumental credited to Don Santiago Jiménez, his father, one of the pioneers of modern conjunto. That led to meeting Don Santiago and posing for a photo with him alongside Billy Gibbons of ZZ Top and Keith Ferguson of the Fabulous Thunderbirds. They got it too.

Santiago Jiménez spoke of the German, Czech, and Polish bands he eavesdropped on at dances around New Braunfels and San Antonio when he was growing up. They were only influences, he said. But Don Santiago couldn't have copied them even if he'd wanted to. Blood and culture turned the same song into something completely different.

As my command of the language improved, so did my appreciation of conjunto's depth and resonance. I realized those mesmerizing melodies that sucked me in were mere embellishments decorating the dramatic songs being performed. That rang especially true for *corridos,* historical accounts of notable people and events told with a take that's usually different from the official history, and *boleros,* the eloquent ballads of romance that underscore why Spanish is the loving tongue.

Further exposure made it obvious that conjunto was a thriving subculture that extended far beyond the musicians and their audience. Venues are essential. If not for bars like Lerma's on Zarzamora Street on San Antonio's west side and institutions such as Juan Tejeda's Guadalupe Cultural Arts Center, where preservation is a conscious part of the presentation, and rural dance halls hewn of sheet metal that seem to have been around forever, conjunto would have gone extinct by now. A similar vital role is played by small Mom-and-Pop record shops such as Janie's and Del Bravo, which is owned by the great *corridista* Salomé Gutiérrez. Mom-and-Pops not only carry a far more extensive selection of CDs and tapes than the chains and supercenters do; they also function as community centers and cool places to hang out. If not for them, there would be no scene.

Recording facilities such as ZAZ Studios, Joey López's hit factory where bands can record one day and walk out with finished product the next, bar code and all, are the real star-making *máquina* of conjunto. And if not for stations like Ricardo Dávila's KEDA-AM, Radio Jalapeño, the best all-conjunto radio station in the whole world, how would the word get out? Fortunately, Ricky not only owns the station, but pulls the morning shift under the guise of Güero Polkas, the screaming, shouting bilingual disc jockey who is a major force promoting conjunto.

Somewhere down the line, the music's ties to the language and the culture, and how both have infused the music with a sense of pride and honor, as well as pleasure, soaked in.

My curiosity eventually led to the living room of Narciso Martínez, El Huracán del Valle, the father of modern conjunto who articulated the melody that blended accordion and bajo sexto. Martínez lived with his wife in a colonia west of Brownsville, a stone's throw from the Rio Grande, Tamaulipas, Mexico, and Latin America. Don Narciso cut a string of tracks for Bluebird beginning in the 1930s and was a pioneering crossover by virtue of recording some polkas under the pseudonyms of Louisiana Pete and Polish Joe to better sell to the Cajun and traditional polka public.

Bruno Villarreal, the blind accordionist credited with making the first conjunto recordings in the 1920s, had departed this earth before I could find him. That missed opportunity has been compensated by being able to witness on numerous occasions the genius of Esteban Jordán, El Parche, the pirate/hippie/jazz cat with an eyepatch who originated a 1960s style described on one recording as *acordeón psicodélico.* He is hardly the only character in the realm. With band names like Los Test Tube Babes and Los Tall Boys, acts like Cuatitos Cantú, accordion-playing dwarf twins each with six-fingered hands, and people like Wally Gonzales, whose hilarious imitation of an Anglo highway patrolman speaking English made his 1970s hit "El Ticketito" a classic, and Snicky Nick Villarreal, who built a career on the phrase "not to worry," there's plenty of color to go around.

One key reason conjunto didn't completely assimilate and disappear as *mexicano-tejanos* morphed into *americanos* is Valerio Longoria, another accordion *maestro* who introduced vocals and romance boleros to the genre. In the early 1990s, Longoria started teaching conjunto accordion to children and adults, sponsored by the Guadalupe Cultural Arts Center. The classes effectively assured the passage of knowledge and tradition to a new generation of conjunto players that includes women, kids, and people with no Mexican blood whatsoever.

This is as good as music gets: a sound that's underground, out of the purview of the mainstream, made for pleasure, not for profit; and a window to a culture that is rich, colorful, exotic yet strangely familiar, as John Dyer so deftly documents in these pages. His subjects include crossover stars, lesser-known *maestros* living in relative obscurity, and all sorts in between. On the surface, conjunto music may appear to be a simple pleasure that serves as an excuse for a people of a certain place and culture to get together and have a good time. But look deep into the eyes of the people in these pictures. They all tell you conjunto is more than that. For them, conjunto is life.

Narciso Martínez, El Huracán del Valle. This "Hurricane of the Valley" played under the names Louisiana Pete and Polish Joe early in his career to better sell to the Cajun and traditional polka public.

PORTRAITS

ALBERTO MACÍAS is son and heir to the late, great master craftsman and *bajo sexto* maker, Martín Macías. From his small shop on the south side of San Antonio, Alberto makes what many musicians consider to be the best hand-crafted *bajo sextos* in the world. He also makes his own hand-wound bronze strings. Learning the trade from his father in the 1950s, Alberto is now handing down the tradition to his son, Jorge, and grandson, Cristóbal.

EVA YBARRA, pictured here at her home in San Antonio, is a multi-instrumentalist, vocalist, composer, recording artist, and teacher. She is considered to be the best female button accordionist in the history of conjunto music and was inducted into the Conjunto Music Hall of Fame in 2002.

FLACO JIMÉNEZ is conjunto music's most renowned world ambassador. A five-time Grammy Award winner (more than any other conjunto or Tejano musician), he has performed throughout Europe, as well as in Australia and Japan. During his fifty-plus years as a musician, he has recorded prolifically, including with such superstars as the Rolling Stones, Bob Dylan, Carlos Santana, Willie Nelson, and the Texas Tornadoes.

Voy a cantarles a los casados
los que les gusta el amor tapado,
allá en la casa toditos buenos
y ellos con otras muy abrazados.

Esta es la moda, y no me admiro,
a mí me gusta también el ruido
pero mi amigo la anda regando
con esa güera que anda trompeando.

La trae del brazo, la anda luciendo
y allá en la casa se están muriendo
porque no llega con la platita
y allá la güera muy bien vestida.

Esta la historia de los casados,
los que les gusta el amor tapado,
amor bonito, amor volado
y si es ajeno, pues más morado.

In this twist on the usual cheating song, a man

chides his friend and other fellow married

men for leaving their wives and families at

home penniless while they paint the town red

with their well-dressed, kept lovers.

Sé que estás pedida y dada
y que te vas a casar
con uno que era mi amigo
y ahora será mi rival.

Los besos y los abrazos
que me diste y que te di
guárdaselos a tu amante
pa' que se acuerde de mí.

Cada vez que paso y miro
por ese dicho lugar,
ya parece que te miro
parece que te oigo hablar.

Los besos y los abrazos
te los voy a regresar,
pa' que nunca se te olvide
a quien vas a abandonar.

In this bittersweet and slightly threatening
reflection on lost love and memory, a man
speaks to his former girlfriend who is marrying
his friend and soon-to-be rival. The singer
vows to return to her all the kisses and
embraces she gave him, so that she will never
be able to forget the one she has left behind.

SANTIAGO JIMÉNEZ JR., son of the late, great Santiago Jiménez Sr. and brother to Flaco, plays the accordion in the traditional style of his father. He has been nominated three times for a Grammy and is the recipient of the National Heritage Award from the National Endowment for the Arts, which honors the nation's significant folk artists.

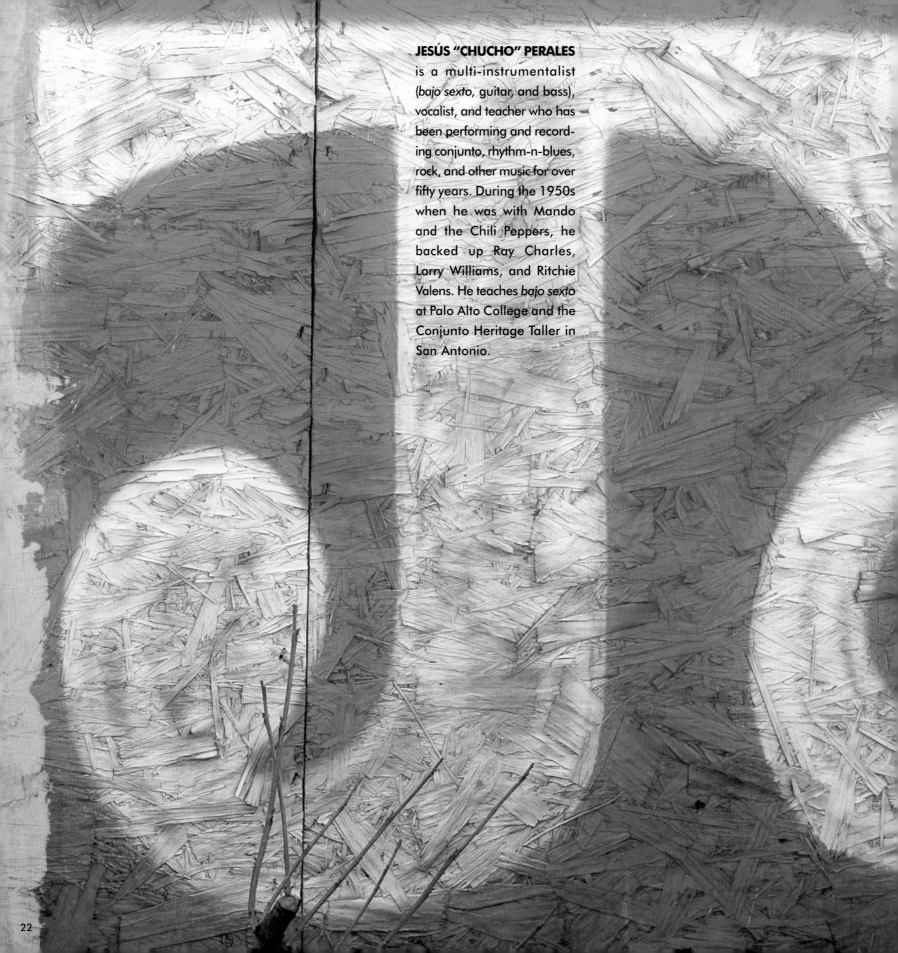

JESÚS "CHUCHO" PERALES is a multi-instrumentalist (*bajo sexto,* guitar, and bass), vocalist, and teacher who has been performing and recording conjunto, rhythm-n-blues, rock, and other music for over fifty years. During the 1950s when he was with Mando and the Chili Peppers, he backed up Ray Charles, Larry Williams, and Ritchie Valens. He teaches *bajo sexto* at Palo Alto College and the Conjunto Heritage Taller in San Antonio.

ÁNGEL FLORES first picked up the accordion at the age of fourteen in his native Corpus Christi. Influenced by the ever-popular Tony de la Rosa, he went on to form his conjunto, Los Alacranes, which became one of the tightest and busiest conjuntos in the nation during the 1970s, '80s, and into the '90s. He first recorded with Discos Nopal in Alice, Texas, and went on to record with Discos Falcón, Freddie Records, Joey Records, and Hacienda Records. His biggest hits have been "Tírame al león" and "El muro."

COMO

By Angel Flores

Como, . . . como te enredaste entre mis manos,
Como te aferraste aquí en mi pecho,
Como me robaste el corazón.

Como, . . . como pudo ser, no me di cuenta,
Cuando platicábamos a solas,
Esa era toda tu intención.

Como, . . . como voy a hacer para explicarte,
Que mi corazón ya tiene amante,
Es una imposible tu intención.

Como, . . . como pudo ser, no me di cuenta
Cuando platicábamos a solas,
Esa era toda tu intención . . .
(Se Repite)

Como, . . . como te enredaste aquí en mis manos
Etc.

"Como" is an exploration of how complicated love can be. A man wonders how a woman to whom he was just talking ended up in his arms and in his heart, which already belongs to another, and agonizes over how he will tell her that this new love can never be.

in love, a man tells his bride that if he had two

hearts himself, he would give them both to her.

Tú fuiste mi consentida desde que te conocí
y así vienes de alto cielo destinada para mí.

De esos dos corazoncitos me mandas uno pa' 'trás
me mandas tu vida entera para amarte más y más.

Qué lindos son dos amores cuando se aman de verdad
se entregan dos corazones para no olvidarse más.

FRED ZIMMERLE was playing the guitar, *bajo sexto*, and accordion by age ten. He began recording in 1945, and in 1950, when he was nineteen years old, he recorded his first 78 rpm record for RCA, and was among the first Spanish language artists in the world to record an album for RCA. He is an accomplished musician and composer whose music has been included in the films *Breathless* and *Nadine*.

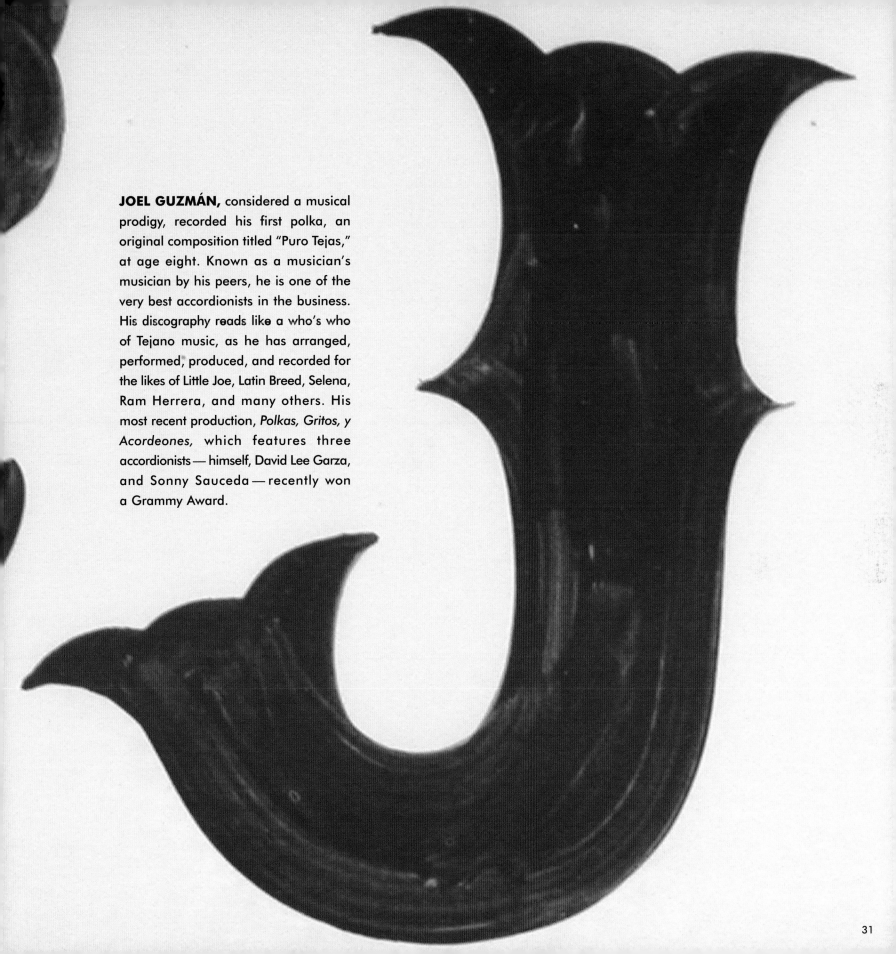

JOEL GUZMÁN, considered a musical prodigy, recorded his first polka, an original composition titled "Puro Tejas," at age eight. Known as a musician's musician by his peers, he is one of the very best accordionists in the business. His discography reads like a who's who of Tejano music, as he has arranged, performed, produced, and recorded for the likes of Little Joe, Latin Breed, Selena, Ram Herrera, and many others. His most recent production, *Polkas, Gritos, y Acordeones,* which features three accordionists — himself, David Lee Garza, and Sonny Sauceda — recently won a Grammy Award.

NICK VILLARREAL is an accomplished singer and accordion stylist, but his greatest contribution to conjunto music is as a songwriter who deals with popular, insightful, and oftentimes hilarious themes and lyrics. He has an uncanny knack for capturing the local, bilingual, Tex-Mex lingo in such songs as "La I-Gotta-Go" and "Kool Aid con Hielo."

LYDIA MENDOZA is one of the most popular and highly acclaimed Tejana singers and instrumentalists of all time. Born in Houston in 1916, she made her first recordings with the Cuarteto Carta Blanca in 1928. In 1934, she recorded one of her greatest hits, "Mal hombre," on the Bluebird label. During the 1950s she recorded with various labels including Columbia and Victor, and she toured Japan, Mexico, South America, and the U.S. In 1976, she was featured in the classic border music film *Chulas Fronteras*. In 1982 she was awarded the National Heritage Award, and in 1999 President Clinton awarded her the National Medal of the Arts.

AMOR DE MADRE

By Lydia Mendoza

Dame por Dios tu bendición
oh madre mía adorada
que yo a tus pies, pido perdón
por lo que tú has sufrido.

En la mansión donde tú estás
una mirada te pido,
madre querida,
ruega por mí al creador.

Tú que estás en la mansión
de este trono celestial
mándale a mi corazón
un suspiro maternal.

Un suspiro maternal
mándale a mi corazón
que me llegue, que me llegue
al corazón.

Mira, madre, que en el mundo
nadie te ama como yo
mira que el amor de madre
estará entre los dos.

Mira, madre, que en el mundo
nadie te ama como yo
se acabó el amor de madre
que era toda mi ilusión.

In this beautiful tribute to her deceased mother,

the singer recalls their shared love and asks

her mother to offer a sign that she is still

watching over her daughter and guiding her

life from on high.

DOS PALOMITAS

By Valerio Longoria

Yo tengo dos palomitas que por ahí andan volando
Son dos lindas trigueñitas que me andan enamorando
Hasta sus alitas abren cuando a mí me oyen cantando.

Una se viste de rosa, otra se viste de blanco
Y se ponen tan celosas que lloran amargo llanto
Como son tan cariñosas a las dos les estoy cantando.

En aquella ventanita se asoma una bella dama
Y al mirarla tan bonita el corazón se me inflama
Como que hace una señita, claro está que a mí me llama.

Yo soy como el huizachito, creciendo y echando flores,
No porque me vean solito, piensan que no sé de amores
A mí me gustan toditas, yo no distingo colores.

Dichoso vive Cupido, dentro de un jardín de flores
Pero más dichoso yo que vivo de los amores
Y a pesar de ser tan pobre, disfruto de las mejores.

Two doves compete for their keeper's attention

in this fresh take on the life of a player.

Armed with desire and love enough for both,

he neglects neither.

VALERIO LONGORIA is considered one of the geniuses of conjunto music. A pioneer accordionist who began playing in the 1930s, he is credited with introducing vocals (the *canción ranchera* sung in polka or waltz time) and the *bolero* into the tradition. Composer, innovator, recording artist, reed tuner, and winner of the National Heritage Award, he developed a new style of playing the accordion that would influence all future generations of accordion players.

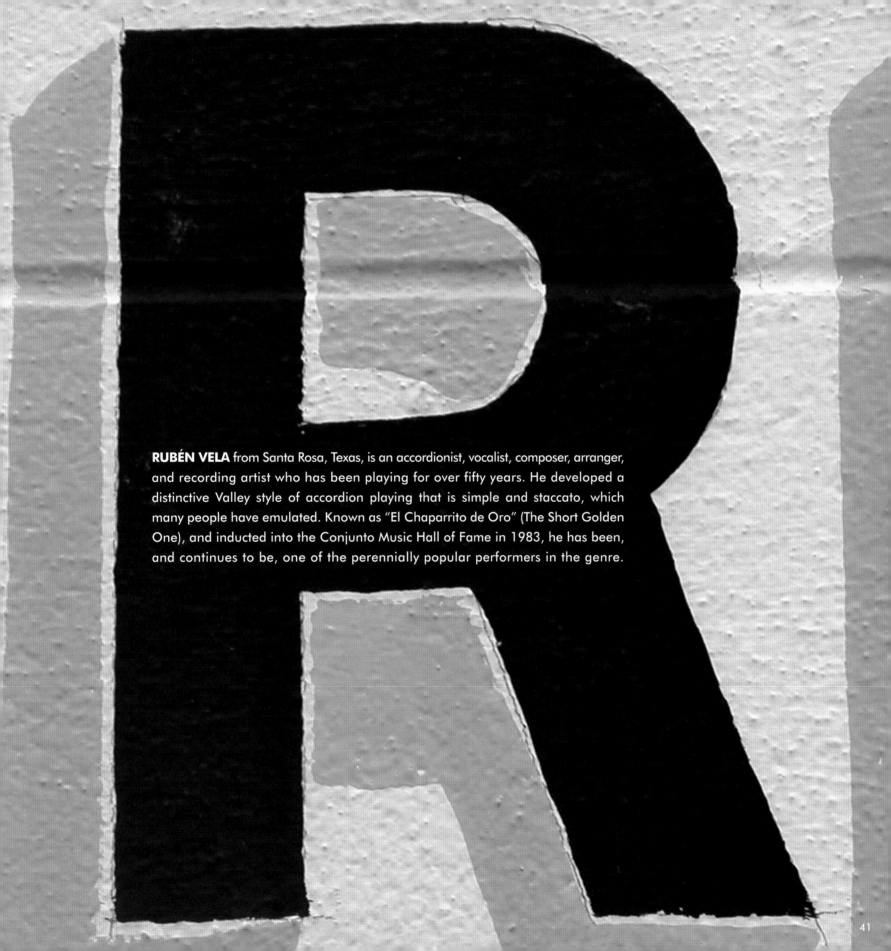

RUBÉN VELA from Santa Rosa, Texas, is an accordionist, vocalist, composer, arranger, and recording artist who has been playing for over fifty years. He developed a distinctive Valley style of accordion playing that is simple and staccato, which many people have emulated. Known as "El Chaparrito de Oro" (The Short Golden One), and inducted into the Conjunto Music Hall of Fame in 1983, he has been, and continues to be, one of the perennially popular performers in the genre.

EL DUETO CARTA BLANCA DE GEORGE Y MAGUE OROSCO is a rare husband-and-wife vocal duet who began singing together in California and upon their return to San Antonio were recorded by Joey "Canelo" López on Cometa Records in 1966. During the 1970s they went on a U.S.O. tour to Germany, Italy, and Austria to entertain the servicemen who craved a bit of down-home Tejano culture. They continue recording and performing for local and regional audiences.

QUE TAL SI TE VAS CONMIGO

By Felipe Martínez
Recorded by George and Mague Orosco

Qué tal si te vas conmigo, aunque no tengas permiso
al cabo soy hombrecito, para echarme el compromiso
ya tienes la edad cumplida, tu mamá ya me lo dijo.

Yo ya no quiero esperarme, ¿por qué no te vas conmigo?
al cabo si tú me quieres, formaremos nuestro nido
no le hace que tus parientes, no te quieran ver conmigo.

Qué tal si te vas conmigo, aunque sea una temporada
ya me soltaron el chisme, de que tú fuiste casada
por eso no te preocupes, a mí no me importa nada.

Si tus parientes se oponen a que tú seas mi querida
dicen que males y vicios no duran toda la vida
vámonos prieta querida, tú serás mi consentida.

"So what if you come away with me?" a man

asks his lover, encouraging her to flout the

tradition of parental consent. Even though it

is rumored that she has been married before,

he says he doesn't care, he only wants her to

be his love.

Con la ropa que te pones y mirar que estás más joven
me dan celos y me pones a pensar
que quizá ya estoy muy viejo y me vas a
        cambiar por otro
otro menso pa' que agarre mi lugar.

Hace tiempo que te quiero decir algo
aunque es cierto que de plano ya estoy pardo
este burro viejo nunca ha rebuznado
tú no más échale carga al burro pardo.

No sé dónde has agarrado, que parezca burro pardo
te equivocas, vas a ver de aquí pa' el real
yo no más quiero que sepas que la edad no
        es la que cuenta
yo he de estirar tu carreta y muchas más.

Hace tiempo que te quiero decir algo
aunque es cierto que de plano ya estoy pardo
este burro viejo nunca se ha rajado
tú no más échale carga al burro pardo.

His old gray burro can still pull his weight,

an aging man tells his wife, whose fondness

for youthful dress and appearance are making

him think she's looking to replace him.

GILBERTO PÉREZ started playing the accordion when he was twenty years old and began his professional career with Rubén Vela. In 1959 he formed his own conjunto and that same year he recorded his first single on Discos Falcón, "El día de la boda." Since 1961 he has been active on the Tejano conjunto circuit and has toured throughout the northern and southwestern United States, taking this music to places it had never been before. Gilberto Pérez y sus compadres are purveyors of a unique Valley style of playing and singing and recognize the importance of conjunto music as a means of instilling cultural pride among Chicanos and mexicanos.

LUPITA RODELA, originally from Schoolland, Texas, and blind since birth, has been playing the accordion and singing for over thirty years, since the age of twelve. Encouraged by Flaco Jiménez, she is one of a handful of female artists to front her own band, Lupita Rodela y su conjunto.

FREDDIE GÓMEZ is an influential Valley musician and vocalist who integrated his distinctive bass and electric guitar accompaniment into conjunto music. In the 1960s he fronted his own band, Freddie Gómez y los Dinámicos, then teamed up with accordionist Rubén Vela to produce various regional hits including "No supe comprender" and "Madrecita." He is a member of the South Texas Conjunto Hall of Fame and was voted "Bass Player of the Century."

CHANO CADENA formed his first conjunto in Alice, Texas, in 1954, and made his first recording, "El cristal polka," in 1955. He developed a distinctive style of playing the accordion that made him very popular throughout the state during the 1960s and '70s, and he was a major musical influence on Rubén Naranjo y los Gamblers. He continues performing and recording and has had several regional hits with Ruby Franco on vocals.

Es la historia de siempre, un amor que se fue
y yo espero mañana comenzar otra vez . . .
sin rencor ni temores, quiero vivir en paz
quiero encontrar mi suerte y no dejarla jamás . . .

Siento que me desgarras el alma entera
ya no me sacrifiques sin la razón.
O es que por ti no pasan las primaveras,
que son las que ablandecen el corazón.

Siento en el alma rota un dolor profundo
que no puedo arrancarlo de mi existir,
ahora pienso en las copas y que en el mundo
todo está preparado para sufrir.

Heartbroken and soul sick, a man sings to

the woman for whose love he vows to wait.

He tells her that no other woman will ever

be the mistress of his heart.

GILBERTO GARCÍA and his longtime *bajista*, RUBÉN GARZA, of LOS DOS GILBERTOS, have been one of the most acclaimed and popular conjuntos of all time. In the 1970s their stylized accordion playing and vocal duet garnered them a huge hit with "El rosalito" which propelled them into a thirty-year-plus recording and performing career that has kept them at the top of the conjunto scene.

HENRY ZIMMERLE, one of the famous Zimmerle family of musicians in San Antonio that includes Henry Sr., Fred, and Nick Villarreal, is a vocalist, guitarist, and *bajo sexto* player who has performed and recorded with such conjunto luminaries as Flaco Jiménez and Salvador García. Henry Zimmerle y su conjunto San Antonio have over 100 recordings to their credit, and he continues to delight audiences with his unique vocal stylings.

EDDIE "LALO" TORRES and his brother, Salvador García, formed the legendary conjunto Los Pavos Reales during the 1950s. An accomplished accordionist and composer, Eddie has performed and recorded prolifically with some of the top conjunto and Tejano artists in the business, including Isidro "El Indio" López, Randy Garibay, and Henry Zimmerle.

POR TI SOY FELIZ

By Salomé Gutiérrez R.
Recorded by Eddie "Lalo" Torres

Llegastes a mí como una canción
Le diste mil dichas a mi corazón
Trajiste la paz aquí a mi vivir,
Por ti soy dichoso, por ti soy feliz.
    (Estribillo)
Contigo supe de lo hermoso de las flores,
Su perfume y sus colores, bajo de ese cielo azul
Por vez primera vi la luna y las estrellas
Tan hermosas y tan bellas, igualitas como tú.

Ni todo es dolor, . . . ni todo es gozar . . .
Si tuvo principios, tendrá su final . . .
Tal vez yo me iré, tal vez te irás
Pero mientras viva yo te he de adorar.
    (Se Repite)
Contigo supe de lo hermoso de las flores
Etc.

A woman has brought happiness, peace,

and a heightened awareness of life's beauty

to the singer in this paean to the power of

love. He vows to love her until he dies, even

if they should part.

Ahora sí me saqué de mi pecho
niña consentida no tenías derecho
a jugar con mi vida,
porque siempre juguete era yo
y tú muy creída me jugaste chueco.

Quisiste hacer de mi vida
lo que a ti te hicieron
cuando en otros tiempos

"Just because others have toyed with you,

you don't have a right to play around with my

life," a man tells his cheating lover. And then

he reminds her that eventually she'll have to

pay for her actions.

ROBERTO PULIDO is one of the most popular and durable top sellers in the history of Tejano music. Together with his band, Los Clásicos, Pulido forged a new synthesis between conjunto and *orquesta* music with his combination of an accordion with two saxophones to pave the way for the Tejano explosion of the 1980s and '90s.

PAULINO BERNAL is an accordionist, vocalist, recording artist, and innovator who during the 1950s and '60s fronted the Conjunto Bernal, which has been called "the greatest and the only one of its kind." Paulino Bernal and the Conjunto Bernal expanded the parameters of conjunto music by introducing the chromatic accordion and three-part vocal harmonies into the genre, as well as integrating styles not normally associated with conjunto music such as *valses peruanos, mariachi sones,* rock, and jazz. Over the last thirty years he has continued performing and recording in his inimitable style the songs that deal with his Christian ministry.

BROTHERS GENARO and **EMILIO AGUILAR,** of **LOS AGUILARES,** have been performing and recording for over forty years. Their pioneering progressive conjunto, which combines keyboard with the accordion and distinctive vocal harmonies, ranks them as one of the elite conjuntos to come out of San Antonio.

JOHNNY DEGOLLADO, "El Montópolis Kid," began playing the accordion in the 1940s and has been a mainstay and institution in the Austin and Central Texas conjunto music scene for over forty-five years. One of the reasons for his long-lasting popularity is his widely acclaimed ability as a songwriter and composer of instrumental music. Many of his over 150 compositions, which include the classic "Te regalo el corazón," have been recorded by some of the top conjuntos in the business, including Los Dos Gilbertos and Rubén Vela y su conjunto.

EL PINTOR

By Johnny Degollado

Yo soy un pintor, cada que yo pinto
pinto unos ojitos, que me hacen llorar.
Yo me siento triste por esa mujer
que desde muy chico empecé a querer.

Esta era una joven, que yo amaba tanto
y la muy ingrata ni se despidió.
Se me fue muy lejos, no sé dónde está
si Diosito quiere, un día volverá.

Qué bonito es su modo de hablar
qué bonito es su modo de andar
cada que yo pinto, pinto sus ojitos
que son luceritos de la oscuridad.

In this song, a painter recalls through his

art his first young love, from whom fate

separated him.

By Domingo "Mingo" Saldívar

Soy como el pájaro negro
mi destino fue fatal
la prenda que más quería
ya abandonó su nidal
vamos los dos por el mundo sin podernos consolar.

Pájaro negro sin suerte
tu pájara se alejó
te acompaño en tus pesaras
lo mismo a mí me pasó
vente, vamos a buscarlas
que sin ellas no más, no.

Pájaro, pájaro negro
anda avisarle a mi amor
que todavía la quiero
que no he olvidado su amor
Pájaro, pájaro negro, si me hicieras el favor.

Separated from his woman and unconsolable,

the singer laments his fate and begs a

blackbird to seek out his beloved and tell

her that he remembers her and still loves her.

DOMINGO "MINGO" SALDÍVAR is one of the most dynamic and expressive accordionists and performers in conjunto music. Known as "The Dancing Cowboy," Mingo slings his accordion low, gyrates, and kicks up his boot heels as he plays and sings. A performer for over forty-five years, Mingo is influential in the crossover between country music and conjunto, having recorded such hits as the bilingual remakes of Johnny Cash's "Ring of Fire" ("Rueda de fuego") and "Folsom Prison Blues" ("La última milla").

LAURA CANALES was known as the undisputed "Reina de la Onda Tejana" (Queen of Tejano Music) during the early-to-mid-1980s, when for four consecutive years she won Female Vocalist and Entertainer of the Year at the Tejano Music Awards. Originally from Kingsville, Texas, she performed with the Conjunto Bernal in 1974 before joining Snowball & Co., then forming her own group, Laura Canales y Encanto, in 1981. For over twelve years she was one of the most consistently successful female performers in Tejano music with one of the most distinctive, powerful, and sensual voices in the history of the genre.

BENE MEDINA is a master accordionist, multi-instrumentalist, and recording artist who has gone largely unrecognized even though he possesses tremendous musical knowledge and talent. El Conjunto de Bene Medina had their first hit record in 1967 with "En cada vida," and his career has spanned the course of nearly five decades. For many years now he has been passing on the conjunto tradition by teaching accordion, first at Alamo Music Center, and most recently with the students at the Conjunto Heritage Taller (pictured here).

By José A. Morante
Recorded by Bene Medina

En cada vida hay un momento
que no se olvida jamás, jamás
y tú, inocente de este cariño,
eres la dicha que he de adorar.

Llegaste a mi alma como un lucero,
del alto cielo te vi caer
y me llenaste el pensamiento
de luz y encanto linda mujer.

No seas ingrata luz de mis ojos
que ya por siempre mi alma estará
que ni la muerte si ahora llegara,
este momento lo arrancará.

Si puedes darme de tu cariño
lo más pequeño que existe en ti,
una migaja como a un mendigo
seré dichoso, seré feliz.

In every life, there is a moment that you

never forget. For this singer, it is the moment

that a beautiful woman came into his life

like heavenly light, filling him with joy and

making him a happy man.

MUJER SIN ALMA

By Pedro Rocha
Recorded by Toby Torres

Todo lo sé, . . . ya no vuelvas a buscarme
nunca pensé . . . que tú fueras a engañarme,
mala mujer, . . . con lo que fuiste a pagarme, . . .
no tienes alma, has herido el corazón.

Voy a vagar, . . . para ver si así me olvido
y no recordar que jamás te he conocido
quiero olvidar, para siempre tu cariño . . .
para que deje de sufrir mi corazón.

Adiós mujer, para siempre me despido
fuiste muy cruel, pero yo no te maldigo
pídele a Dios que perdone tu pecado,
para que tu alma no se vaya a condenar.

Voy a vagar para ver si así me olvido
y no recordar que jamás te he conocido
quiero olvidar, para siempre tu cariño . . .
para que deje de sufrir mi corazón.

"Don't come looking for me, you soulless, cheating woman," he tells her. "I want to forget about you and all the suffering you caused me."

TORIBIO "TOBY" TORRES began playing the *bajo sexto* at age fourteen and during the 1950s was performing with Conjunto Maravilla and Valerio Longoria, among many others. A masterful *bajista* in the traditional style, he has taught many students to play *bajo,* and in the 1970s opened up his own recording studio (first ZAZ Records, then Toby's Custom Recording Studio) where he recorded Flaco Jiménez's Grammy Award winning "Ay te dejo en San Antonio," as well as records by many other musicians including Tito Guizar, Frank Rodarte, and Doug Sahm.

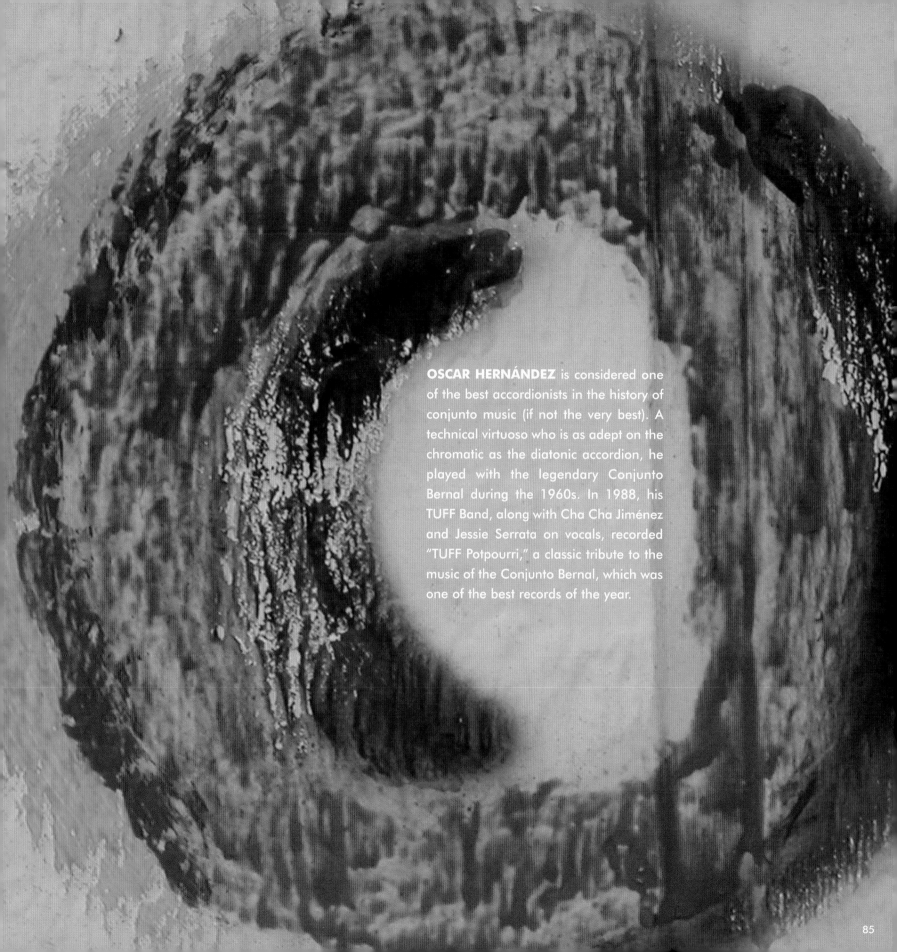

OSCAR HERNÁNDEZ is considered one of the best accordionists in the history of conjunto music (if not the very best). A technical virtuoso who is as adept on the chromatic as the diatonic accordion, he played with the legendary Conjunto Bernal during the 1960s. In 1988, his TUFF Band, along with Cha Cha Jiménez and Jessie Serrata on vocals, recorded "TUFF Potpourri," a classic tribute to the music of the Conjunto Bernal, which was one of the best records of the year.

SALOMÉ GUTIÉRREZ is a songwriter and composer of *corridos*, owner of Del Bravo Record Shop (pictured here), DLB Records, and San Antonio Music Publishing. In his small studio he has recorded some of conjunto music's all-time greats, including Valerio Longoria, Daniel Garcés, Flaco Jiménez, Rubén Naranjo, Salvador García, and many others. A consummate businessman who has been creating, producing, and promoting Texas-Mexican music for over fifty years, he is a longtime member of the Tejano Music Hall of Fame.

DANIEL GARCÉS played the guitar and sang with his Conjunto Los Tres Reyes during the 1940s and '50s; however, he is best known as a gifted songwriter who composed some of the most memorable standards in Tejano music, including "Mujer paseada," "Los pizcadores," "Dilema de los dos," and "No nos quieren, corazón." Many of his more than two hundred original songs were popularized in Mexico and throughout Latin America.

MI DESVENTURA

By Daniel Garces

Llorando la obsesión de tu recuerdo
me alejo para siempre de tu vida
de aquel amor que fué mentira.
    (Puente)
Murieron mis más bellas ilusiones
hoy vivo cautivado en mi amargura
de aquel amor que unió dos corazones
tan solo queda mi desventura.

Qué importa mi amargura y mi dolor,
si en ti logré encontrar felicidad,
si tú ya eres feliz con otro amor
que yo sufra por ti, que más me da . . .

Los días para mí pasan muy tristes
en cambio para ti son días felices
y mientras ríes tú, yo estoy llorando
por el engaño que a mi alma hiciste

A cheating woman leaves behind a man

who passes his days disconsolate and

sorrowful over the beautiful dreams that

her lies shattered.

ME IMPORTA MADRE

By Salvador T. García

Me importa Madre que tú ya no me quieras,
Ya me han contado que sales con cualquiera,
Me importa Madre que tú ya no me quieras,
Madre me importa si me quieras o no,
Madre me importa si me quieras o no.

Dices que quieres que yo te perdone,
Que porque quieres regresar conmigo,
Yo ya no quiero tamales de chivo,
Me importa Madre, si regresas o no,
Madre me importa si regresas o no.
    (Bridge)
Me importa Madre si te vas o te quedas,
Qué te diviertas con él que tú quieras,
Me importa Madre si te vas o te quedas,
Madre me importa si me quieras o no
Madre me importa si me quieras o no . . .
Dices que quieres que yo te perdone

"You say that you want me to forgive you,"

he tells her, "but it doesn't matter to me

anymore whether you stay or go, whether

you love me or not."

SALVADOR T. GARCÍA, originally from Seguin, began performing with the conjunto Hermanos García-Torres during the 1940s, and during the 1950s, along with his brother, Eddie "Lalo" Torres, formed the seminal conjunto Los Pavos Reales. He is an accordionist, vocalist, and multi-instrumentalist who is best known for his amazing recording career and original compositions numbering over three hundred.

AMADEO FLORES, inspired by Reynaldo Barrera, learned how to play the *bajo sexto* when he was ten years old. From 1948 to 1955 he was the *bajista* with Tony de la Rosa y el Conjunto de la Rosa, with whom he recorded many of Tony's early popular hits including "El circo," "La grulla," and "Rosa Ana." Around 1954 he taught himself how to play the accordion, and soon thereafter he formed El Conjunto Ideal. Inducted into the Conjunto Music Hall of Fame in 1995, Amadeo is a master accordion tuner and repairman who is much in demand in Alice, Texas.

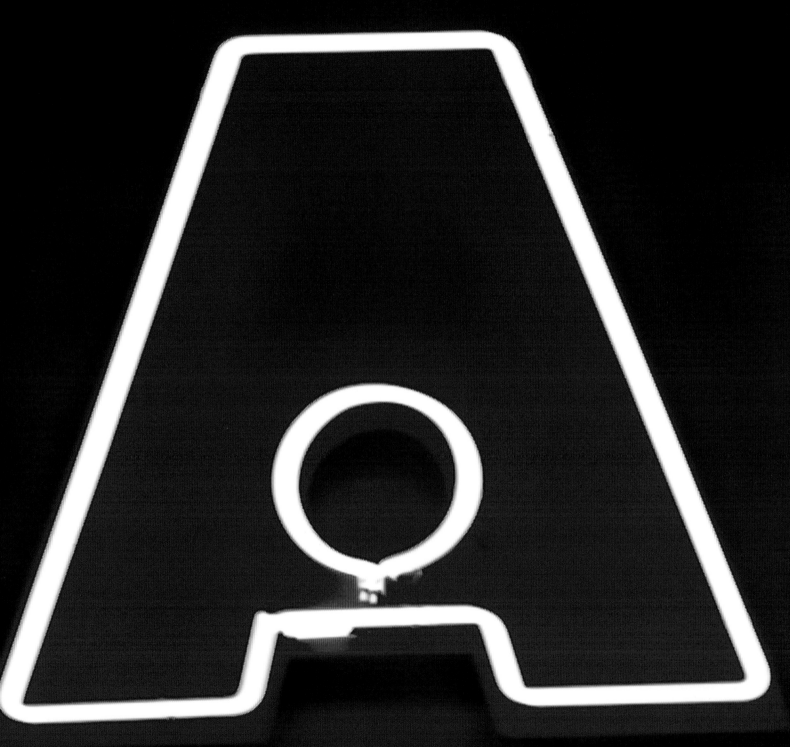

DAVID LEE GARZA and his band Los Musicales are one of the most popular and accomplished bands in Tejano music. Hailing from Poteet, Texas, David Lee has put together a progressive conjunto sound that combines the accordion with saxophone and keyboards. Winner of numerous Tejano Music Awards, the band has also fronted some of the best vocalists in the business, including Ram Herrera, Emilio Navaira, and Jay Pérez.

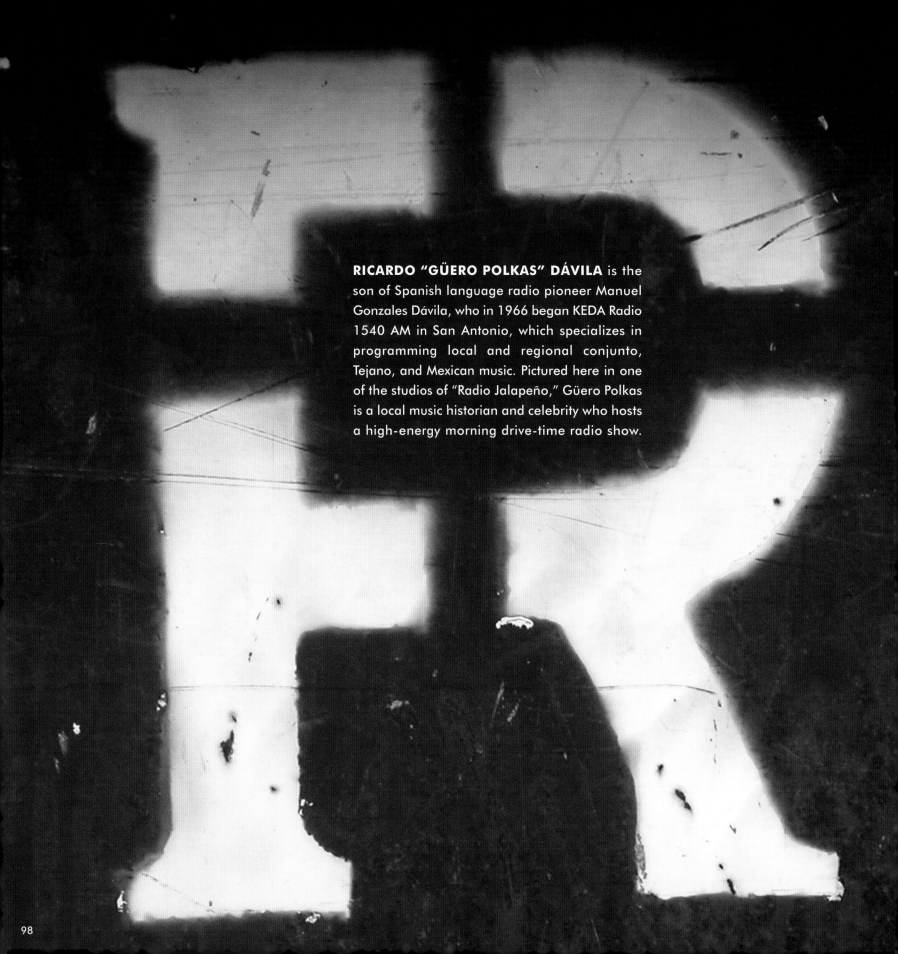

RICARDO "GÜERO POLKAS" DÁVILA is the son of Spanish language radio pioneer Manuel Gonzales Dávila, who in 1966 began KEDA Radio 1540 AM in San Antonio, which specializes in programming local and regional conjunto, Tejano, and Mexican music. Pictured here in one of the studios of "Radio Jalapeño," Güero Polkas is a local music historian and celebrity who hosts a high-energy morning drive-time radio show.

ON THE SCENE

Conjunto music is played nearly everywhere. To the left an itinerant group entertains arriving guests at a quinceañera (a traditional party hosted by the parents of a young girl who has turned fifteen). San Benito, Texas. At right Freddie Gómez's friend, accordionist Juan Tapia, jams with Freddie in his living room near Edinburg, Texas.

At right, Paulino Bernal often invites his friends to his ranch near Edinburg for a day of music and good food and fellowship. Here Paulino starts the music off with his own conjunto and a traditional song on the back porch of the ranch house. Above left, the accordion is the heart and soul of conjunto music. Because it is the lead instrument, it is made in a vast array of brilliant colors and finishes, all designed to catch the eye.

The accordion is a difficult
instrument to learn to play.
Many aspiring musicians are
drawn to it as a symbol of the
driving, romantic, danceable
music of conjunto.

Conjunto music is, above all, dance music. Whole families attend the festivals and dances, alternately eating and drinking and socializing. But it's never too long before they return to the dance floor. At right, Eva Ybarra and her *bajo sexto* player, Chucho Perales, play for the throngs at the Tejano Conjunto Festival held every May at Rosedale Park on the west side of San Antonio.

At left, a hat covered by autographs is a traditional way to collect the signatures of one's favorite musicians. At right, the dance floor is always crowded. Everyone has a favorite musician. When a particularly well-known band begins to play, the audience crowds around the stage to get a better view.

Conjunto music appeals to all ages. Seniors, such as these couples at the Royal Palace Ballroom in San Antonio, regularly attend dances arranged just for them, often in the middle of the afternoon.

There is no correct way to dance to conjunto music. The couples circle the dance floor, weaving in and out, back and forth, in rhythm to the infectious music.

Conjunto dances and festivals are places to see and be seen. Loyalty to certain musicians and bands is evident with the wearing of customized t-shirts, such as this couple on the right who enjoy Roberto Pulido.

Clothing styles at conjunto dances are as varied as the people who wear them. But, even though conjunto music is associated with Texas-Mexican working-class urban folks, western wear is often seen.

ACKNOWLEDGMENTS

Conjunto is an important project, especially culturally. The people in this book deserve to be recognized. Doing the photography was great fun and I loved every minute of it. Overall, the subjects were gracious, hospitable, and helpful. I feel that I have made many new lifelong friends. Conjunto people are like that.

I want to heartily thank a number of folks without whom this book would never have been produced. First and foremost, I want to thank my old friend DJ Stout of Pentagram Design. DJ saw the potential in the photos I had taken over the years and introduced me to the staff at the University of Texas Press. His design for this book is a great example of why he is undeniably the premier book designer anywhere. DJ's designer sidekick Julie Savasky gets a special tip of my hat for putting up with my constant questions and changes of mind. Her input for the design is invaluable. Thanks, Julie.

What can I say about Juan Tejeda and Joe Nick Patoski, who contributed two of the most insightful, warm, informational essays that any photographer could ask for? What can I say but thanks and thanks again. You guys explain why the subject of conjunto is so important.

My thanks also go to Theresa May, assistant director and editor-in-chief of U.T. Press, who immediately realized the importance of this book. She has been a generous, steady, guiding hand throughout the whole book publication process. Her many thoughtful suggestions have made things go so much easier. I also want to thank Dave Hamrick, David Cavazos, Gianna LaMorte, Regina Fuentes, and Carolyn Cates Wylie, U.T. Press staffers all, who were unfailingly positive and helpful.

Lionel Sosa, dean of Hispanic advertising, a dear friend and a real inspiration to us all, introduced me to Jesus Rangel of Anheuser-Busch, whose generosity helped make this book a reality. Las más sinceras gracias a ustedes por todo.

And, most especially, I want to thank my wife, Diane, and my two lovely children, Jonny and Rebecca, who have been there for me through this long, interesting process. Their support and understanding of the importance of this project means so very much to me.

And, once again, a great big gracias to all of you conjunto musicians who allowed me to enter your lives and spend a few moments with you. I will remember these times forever.

John Dyer